T0365361

Buddies

Written and Illustrated by Susan Burg

Print information available on the last page

Rev. date: 09/29/2015

To order additional copies of this book, contact:
Xlibris
1-800-455-039
www.xlibris.com.au
Orders@Xlibris.com.au

This book belongs to

With special thanks to

Jennifer Ridley

The Archer Social Club

The Disability Trust

For helping to make my dreams come true

"Hi everyone, my name is Billy G Crossbow, I am your friendly neighbourhood Grasshopper and I live in a little village called Green Oaks. It's in a far way land called Wimble Womble Land. This is my best buddy Jeffery O'Brien. Do you know what kind of animal he is? Well if you can't guess what kind of animal Jeffery is, he is a strange looking Otter who loves adventure.

Our adventure begins on one fine spring day when the flowers were blooming and the flies were buzzing. I was with my best friend when we spotted some action across the street.

I turned to my friend and said "Hey Jeffery, why is that big blue bug flying around and around? He looks like he's going to land outside that house on the other side of the street. "Wow, all insects are scattering about to stay out of the large blue bugs way. "Can you see those big black letters?" asked Jeffery, I told Jeffery that if he can stop flapping his wings long enough, I will be able read what it says. "Billy G what are you doing?" Jeffery said to me. I told Jeffery that I am trying to hop faster so I can try and read what's written on the bug's wing. "Look Billy G" said Jeffery. "The wings are starting to slow down. I can read what it says now, it says R, E, M, O, V, A, L, I, S, T" spelt Jeffery. "Well Billy G that's a removalist bug" I was amazed, I had never seen a removalist bug before. "I heard whispers from a lot of small insects that they think the house might be haunted? How scary that would be?" I asked. I then noticed a bright purple caterpillar crawling slowly up behind the big blue bug.

A lady green ant and then a man green ant slipped off the big bright purple caterpillar. They opened the bright blue spot at the back of the caterpillar, then a smaller ant crawled out and fell with a big "plop" onto the sandy ground. The man ant then helped him up and led him into their new little home. "Hey look Billy G, he looks about the same age as us" said Jeffery. I then said to Jeffery that we might be able to play with him in the morning. Jeffery then told me about a great idea to get up early tomorrow morning to go and visit the ant family together.

"Come on Jeffery lets go" His dad called out. "Let's go, those fish are not going to wait for us all morning" Jeffery went running after his dad skipping and jumping high into the air, he was so excited. You see, Jeffery likes going fishing with his dad. How many fish do you think they will catch?

Jeffery told his Dad "It looks like a new family is moving into the house across the street." "Oh yes" replied his Dad. "I did see the big Removalist Bug stopping. They look like a nice Green Ant family Jeffery." "Can we go and see them tomorrow?" asked Jeffery "And welcome them to Green Oaks?" "Yes of course we can" agreed his father. "You and Billy G might be able to play with the boy ant. I did see him, when he dropped onto the sandy ground"

The next morning, I hopped through Jeffery's open bedroom window and greeted "Good morning Jeffery, it's time to get up. So rise and shine" Jeffery rolled over in bed and had a big stretch. "Oh hello Billy G, what are you doing here so early?" I had to remind Jeffery that we said we would go over and see if we could play with the new Green Ant Boy and I also added I could not sleep any longer due to having a long stem of wheat tickling me on my face all night. "Why's that Billy G?" asked Jeffery. "Oh I slept at Farmer McGee's barn last night, and also, that pesky rooster kept crowing as loud as he could" I replied.

Jeffery pulled off his blanket and climbed out of bed saying, "Come on Billy G, let's go and get some breakfast. Did you know, it is the most important meal of the day?" I hopped and Jeffery ran down a tunnel that leads into the kitchen. Jeffery's mum was cooking some fish for Jeffery's dad. Jeffery then said, "Wow mum that smells so good" "Would you like some cooked fish too Jeffery?" Mum then replied. "Oh no thank you mum, I would like mine raw thanks. I like raw fish most of all "Jeffery asked me, "Billy G would you like some fish?" "No thanks "I answered. "I don't like fish it gives me a rash and it will leave me with big lumps all over my head" "That sounds disgusting" said Jeffery's mum. I explained to Jeffery's mum that it takes so long for the lumps to go away and how hard it is for me to hop because my head becomes far too heavy.

Jeffery finished off his breakfast then asked me. "Well, are we ready to go and play with the new green ant boy today Billy G?" I stretched my wings into the air and said. "Yes let's go Jeffery". "We could take him fishing, or maybe we will go climbing trees. Come on Billy G lets go" Jeffery said with excitement. We went running and hopping out into Jeffery's backyard, under and over the fence we went. Can you guess which one of us went under the fence? Well it was me, because I don't like hopping too high because I do get these weird head spin's. But, Jeffery is up and over the fence without a problem at all, his a lot bigger then I am.

We carefully crossed the road, looking right and then to the left and then to the right again to make sure nothing was coming. We then walked and hopped quickly and carefully across the road. We walked and hopped up the sandy footpath to the ant family's front door. Jeffery knocked loudly on the door. The door opened, it was the lady green ant and she said, "Hello there, can I help you?" "Um" said Jeffery. "We would like to play with your son, if that is okay with you?" We would also like to welcome you to Green Oaks. I am sorry Mrs Green Ant, my name is Jeffery O'Brien, and this is my best friend and buddy Billy G Crossbow"

"Well come on in Jeffery and Billy G" said Mrs Green Ant. "Lenny is in the sand room reading a book and learning Braille " Jeffery scratched behind his ear and asked Mrs Ant, "What's Braille?" "Well Jeffery" said Mrs Green Ant. "Lenny is visually impaired, and he can't see as well as you and Billy G, Jeffery. Braille is a way that Lenny can read his favourite books. Come on in and meet Lenny, he will be pleased to meet you both. Lenny hasn't had many friends since he started to lose his eyesight and he is quite lonely"

Mrs Green Ant told Jeffery and me that Braille is a series of dots that help someone whom is visually impaired to read.

Can you figure out what Jeffery enjoys doing with his dad using the Braille below?

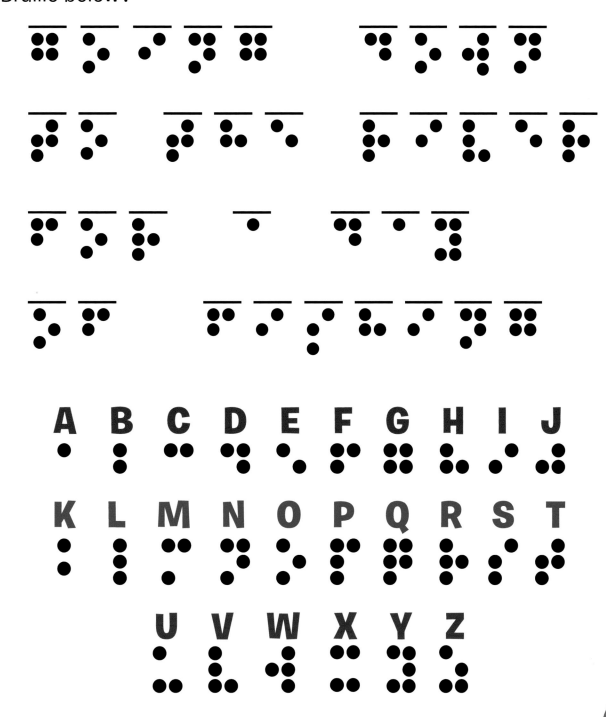

Do you think you could write your name in Braille?

Lenny was sitting on the sand floor reading a book. Mrs Green Ant said the green ant boy. "Lenny, you have some friends here that have come to visit you." Lenny quickly put his book down and stood up. He reached for a long yellow cane which had a blue handle and a blue ball on the tip. As he held the cane in front of him, he rolled it to right and then to the left. As he walked closer to Jeffery and I, he put his hand out so he could shake my wing and Jeffery's paw and said hello.

"Hi Lenny, my name is Billy G Crossbow. The G stands for Grasshopper"
"And my name is Jeffery O'Brien Otter" said Jeffery. "Wow", said
Lenny. "You both certainly have long names. My name is just Lenny
Green Ant"

"That's a great name Lenny" Jeffery said. He then asked "Lenny
would you like to come and play with us?" Lenny replied nervously
"I don't know, you see many animals and insects like to tease me
and bully me where ever I go, so I don't go out much"

"Oh come on Lenny" Jeffery said, "You will be okay with us. Billy G and I will look after you and we can all be good buddies. You have nothing to worry about" Mrs Green Ant overheard the kids and added "It will be fun for you Lenny to go out and play, it would be better than staying inside all day" "But mum, what happens if I get lost?" "You will be fine Lenny" said Jeffery. "We won't leave you alone, you will be okay" "Okay" said Lenny, "I have to put my hat on. I won't be long" Mrs Green Ant said. "Thank you Billy G and Jeffery for taking Lenny out to play. But please be careful that he doesn't get lost or hurt I do worry when he goes out. But I do thank you"

As Jeffery and I waited for Lenny in the hallway for him to get ready, we saw Lenny's cane slide out of a tiny hole in the wall, then Lenny's head appeared with a big 'POP', then the rest of Lenny's body followed. "Are you ready Lenny?" asked Mrs Green Ant. "Yes mum all ready" he replied. All Jeffery could say was. "Cool, great hat Lenny. I really like that colour blue, it really suits you"

Lenny, Jeffery and I walked down the sandy footpath and onto a grassy patch. Jeffery then asked "Well, what we are going to do first Billy G?" Lenny suggested "Can we play a game off hide and seek. You see, I don't even have to put a blind fold on and that makes it easier for me never having to find a clean piece of cloth to put over my eyes. And when I have to seek, I use my cane to feel for insects and other animals. By rolling my cane in front of me, it helps me find things on the ground so I don't trip especially when I go over rocky ground"

Jeffery said. "Come on Billy G and Lenny, let's go and find some more of our buddies, so we can all play together it will be so much fun. We might be able to play hide and seek later." I thought that was a great idea. Jeffery then continued "Let's go down to the big pine tree in the centre of Green Oaks. Most of our buddies hang out around there"

Lenny rolled his cane to the right and then to the left feeling his way across the bumpy ground. I hopped and clicked my wings together as we made our way towards the centre of Green Oaks. Jeffery and I felt very proud as we walked over the bumpy ground. I think it's because we were caring for Lenny and watching out for him, making sure he didn't hurt himself.

"Hey look over there" Jeffery said. "Look who is sitting in the shade of the big old pine tree, its Kayla Red Fox. Come on, let's go and see her, come on Lenny". Then Jeffrey went on to say "Look Billy G, I can also see Corben and Oscar Snail sitting near the big old pine tree as well. Oscar keeps popping in and out of his shell" I told Jeffery that I think it might be because he is getting to hot in the sun.

Jeffery called out to Kayla Red Fox and she came running towards us asking "What are you all doing here?" "Well Kayla" said Jeffery. "We were coming to see if you would like to play with us?" Then, Jeffery said to Kayla "Would you like to meet a new buddy of ours?" "I would love to" Kayla announced showing excitement. Jeffery then called out "Hey Lenny can you make your way over to us? I have someone special for you to meet?"

Lenny peeked out from behind Jeffery and said "Here I am" Kayla glanced at Lenny and said. "Hello Lenny, it's nice to meet you. Wow what is that blue ball on the end of that long cane for Lenny?" "I use the ball as my eyes on the ground to keep a look out for objects, which helps me to not trip over Kayla" Kayla looked puzzled and asked me, "Billy G, what does Lenny need it for?" "Well Kayla, Lenny is visually impaired. He can't see like us and he uses his cane like we use our eyes" Look here comes Corben and Oscar Snail.

"Hello Buddies" Corben and Oscar called out together. "What are you all doing here?" Jeffery then replied "Would you like to come and play with us?" "Ok" said Corben. Kayla said, "You should meet Lenny, he can be a new buddy of ours" "Hi Lenny" said Corben and Oscar. "It's really nice to meet you" I am always so proud of most of my buddies. They are always so polite to our friends and the interesting new people they meet.

The Buddies started a journey together with Kayla singing a little song. The group came across a pond and Kayla stopped singing to tell the group she has found our friend Henry Mosquito. "Yes" Jeffery and I yelled out at the same time. "We can see Henry Mosquito over near the edge of the pond. Come on lets go see if he want to play" When we reached Henry, he was busy swooping in and out of his pond looking for food. Henry looked up, saw us and buzzed. "G'day Buddies what are you doing?" Jeffery waved him over and asked him, if he would like to play?" "Yeah that would be great but who is your new friend?" Kayla explained "This is our new ant buddy Lenny" "Nice to meet you Lenny" said Henry. "By the way, what's that cane with that big blue ball on the end for?" Lenny told Henry how it helped him find his way around. Kayla said. "He is really good with the cane Henry, unfortunately Lenny can't see very well" "Oh" said Henry "Hey buddies, look over there, I can see Ivy Butterfly" said Henry "Let's go say hello"

We hopped, crawled and flew quickly over to see Ivy Butterfly fluttering her bright beautifully coloured wings. She was singing "La, La, De, Dah" while she looked at some lovely flowers. Henry flew up to her and asked "Would you like to come and play with all of your buddies?"

But Ivy didn't hear him. Henry then flew onto Ivy's back and she screamed in fright. She started fluttering her wings which made Henry almost fall off. "Thank goodness that Henry can fly" said Oscar Snail. Ivy turned around and waved her brightly coloured wings. She didn't know that Henry had been talking to her "So sorry Henry, I didn't hear you. You see I can't hear, I am hearing impaired. That's why I am trying to find a Trumpet flower so I can use it to hear" Kayla said "I didn't know you were hearing impaired" "Yes Kayla, since I was in a cocoon, it's not much of a problem now that I have had plenty of practise doing what is called lip reading. Which I watch you speak and I make out words by the movements your mouth makes" Kayla was amazed then said "Come on Ivy and meet

Lenny, he is visually impaired and he is our new buddy, let's all go and play"

"Well I never" said Jeffery as we went around a bend. "It is Chloe and Mason Dragonfly. "Hey, would you like to come and play with us?" Jeffery continued "We were all thinking of maybe going on a march through Green Oaks Forest later as well. Oh by the way this is our new friend Lenny Green Ant. He has just moved into the house across from mine" "Hello Mason and Chloe" said Lenny. Chloe asked "What is that that stick for Lenny?" Lenny answered "It's my cane, I can't see very well and it helps me find any bumps and things that I could trip over" "Wow can I have a play with your cane?" buzzed Mason. "I'm afraid not" said Jeffery "It's not a toy and it's very important to me. Anyway let's go on our march, we are going to have a lot of fun. Come on buddies!"

"Look over there everyone" called Jeffery. "It's Stoop the Great Bull Frog, he always looks grumpy doesn't he?" I said that he always looks like that to me too. "I don't think he can help it Jeffery, because when he is in a good mood and having fun, he doesn't look any different. Come on Lenny come over here with me and meet Stoop"

Lenny used his cane to feel his way across the uneven ground. "Oops, be careful Lenny there are a few holes" said Jeffery. "They are only tiny but still big enough that you could trip on one" "That's ok Jeffery, my cane will help me find the holes" We all raced up to Stoop the Great Bull Frog. "Hey Stoop" called out Jeffery. "Come and meet our new buddy Lenny" Stoop let out a loud grumbly type croak "No I won't, he can't see me, so I am not going to waste my time and energy" "Well " said Jeffery "That is so rude of you Stoop" Stoop let another loud croak and took one large leap into the air and he was gone.

"Never mind Lenny" I said. "You have made some new friends today. Come on lets go on our march, are we all ready?" "Listen everyone" said Lenny. "I can hear someone crying" Jeffery and even I, couldn't hear a thing. Kayla Red Fox said. "No I can't hear anything" Henry and Ivy said. "No we can't either" Chloe and Mason Dragon fly also heard nothing. Then Corben and Oscar Snail said. "We are close to the ground and we can't feel any movement on the ground" Lenny explained, that when he started to lose his eyesight his hearing got a lot better. And he could still hear someone crying and pointed his cane the direction the sound was coming from and said "let's check it out"

"Over here, this way" Lenny said. Everyone followed Lenny as he rolled his cane to the right and then to the left to feel his way through the long grass. "Over here, this way buddies" Jeffery pushed the long green grass to the side and there was Stoop, crying. "What is the matter?" We all asked. Stoop stopped crying long enough to say, "I have lost my red Croaking Stone down a hole when I leaped away from all of you after meeting Lenny" Everyone spoke at once saying, "Show us where you lost it Stoop"

Jeffery said. "I am far too big to get in that hole to reach it" I added that my wings are far too wide and I wouldn't be able to move. Kayla Red Fox said. "I can dig it out, but the sandy ground might fall in on me and that would be dangerous" Henry Mosquito buzzed. "Not me I don't like small places" Ivy said. "I wouldn't hear the sandy ground if it started fall in on me" Then Corben and Oscar said.

"We wouldn't fit because of our shells" Then in a big voice, Lenny said. "I will go" Stoop said in a grumpy tone "You cannot see you wouldn't be able to find my stone" Lenny replied "I'm small enough and will fit into the hole with ease. I can feel my way through with my cane. I will find your Croaking Stone for you Stoop, you just wait and see" Lenny crawled into the hole and felt his way down into the tiny tunnels with his cane.

Lenny found the Croaking Stone and crawled back up the steep tunnel. Lenny's cane appeared through the hole first, followed by Lenny with the Croaking Stone. We all cheered. We were all so happy that Lenny was okay and that he also had found the Croaking Stone. Lenny was Stoop's hero, he was so happy.

Miss July Augustine Spider, who lives in a tree close to the hole spun a new and strong web and then she tied the Croaking Stone around Stoop's neck. Stoop was so happy and he let out the biggest croak "Thankyou Lenny"

Lenny Green Ant now has a lot of new buddies who care for him and help him to lead a normal and fulfilling life. We all thought we better get Lenny home. His mum and dad will be wondering where he is. When we got there, Mrs and Mr Green Ant were waiting outside for Lenny. Lenny said with excitement "I have had such a great day Mum and Dad. I have made a lot of new Buddies and I helped Stoop the Great Bull Frog to find his croaking stone."

The End!

Join the dots to make Billy and his friends?

Billy

Jeffery

The Removalist Bug

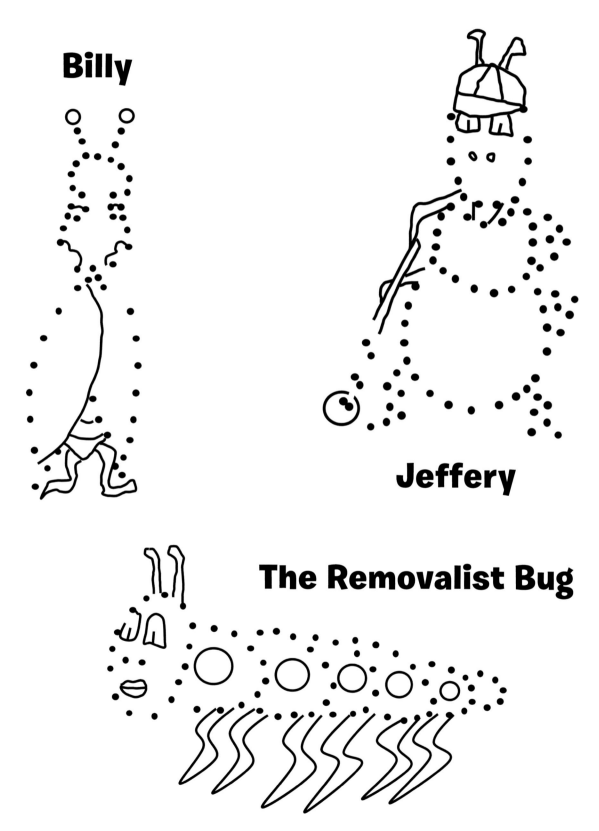

Activities for home

With some of your friends or your buddies put a clean cloth over your eyes and you will feel the same as Lenny. Have your friends put some special thing into a bag and you have 2 guesses what they are. Something's might be easy and some might be hard.

Put a blind fold on and try to walk around a room without peeking. But please make sure that there is nothing that will hurt you. Some of your friends say watch out if you are going bump into something. Be careful.

Susan Burg

Susan was born in Sussex England. She migrated with her family to Australia in 1964. Arriving in Fremantle, they travelled extensively throughout Tasmania and the East Coast, finally settling in Merrylands NSW, where Susan continued her education.

Later, Susan became involved in both the ChildCare and Aged Care industries as well as qualifying in Hospitality Management.

Moving to Bingara in early 2011, Susan started to write her series of children's stories. She started to lose vision in her right eye. Eventually, her vision deteriorated to 5% in her left eye only. Sue now lives in Nowra N.S.W,

By connecting her computer to a wide screen television, Susan has been able to continue writing and illustrating her books.

Email Sue at: susanburg22@yahoo.com.au

Printed in the United States
By Bookmasters